INDIA'S
DISAPPEARING RAILWAYS

A PHOTOGRAPHIC JOURNEY

ANGUS McDONALD

FOREWORD BY SIR MARK TULLY

Opposite: Shakuntala Express, Motibagh, 3 February 2007

GOODMAN
FIELL

Published in 2014 by Goodman Fiell
An imprint of the Carlton Publishing Group
20 Mortimer Street
London W1T 3JW

10 9 8 7 6 5 4 3 2 1

Edited by Catherine Anderson

A CIP catalogue record for this book is available from the British Library.

ISBN 978 1 78313 011 5

Printed in China

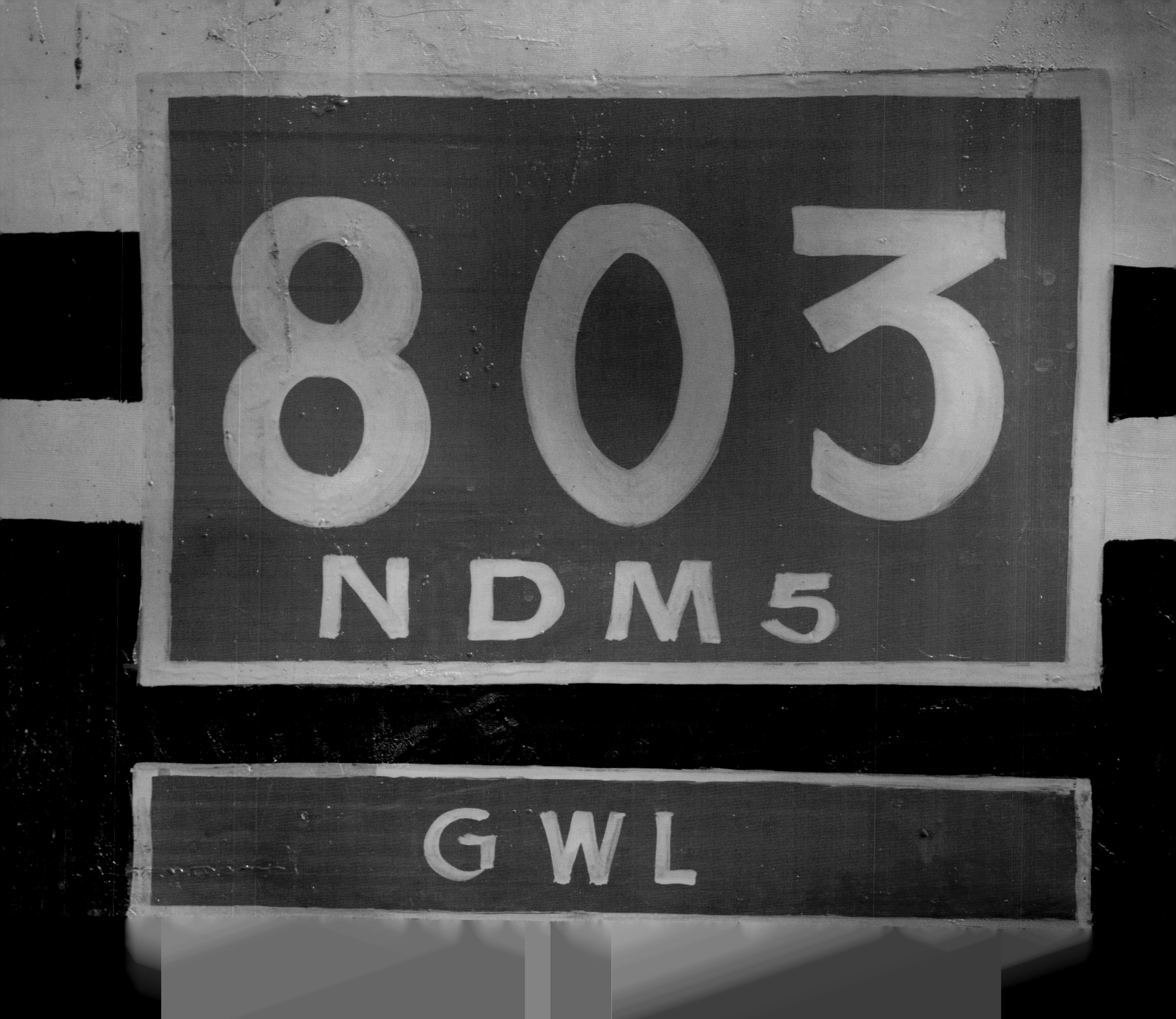
803
NDM5
GWL

Left: Gwalior Light Railway, Sheopur Kalan, 8 March 2011

FOREWORD

Sir Mark Tully

When the imperious Governor General, Lord Dalhousie, decided that India should have railways he also decreed that there should be no repetition of the mistake the British government had made by allowing two different gauges to develop. But even Dalhousie couldn't countermand India's diversity and its cavalier attitude to the dictates of government. How could a land of many religions and languages, a land where different dialects abound, a land whose terrain includes the Himalayas – the world's highest mountains – the fertile green plain of the Ganges, and the barren deserts of Rajasthan, ever be satisfied with just one gauge? And it wasn't. Four different gauges emerged. How could a people who believe laws are there to be broken have accepted Dalhousie's dictate? One of Angus McDonald's photographs illustrates the Indian attitude to laws. On the back of the carriage of a train standing in a station on the Gwalior Light Railway there is a partially obscured notice which, as far as I can tell, reads "Please riding on the roof is forbidden and will attract a fine of 500 rupees or three months in jail". The roof of the carriage is crowded with passengers, some of them happily lending a hand to those still scrambling to get aboard. Angus himself must have done a bit of dangerous law-breaking to shoot the remarkable pictures of another Gwalior train crossing a bridge with a very low clearance and a roof-top crowded with prone passengers.

This is a book about the smaller gauge railways of India, railways which were always lesser than the mighty broad-gauge lines. But they were all built for serious purposes. The Dabhoi railway system was built to transport cotton; the Gwalior Light Railway to carry food to remote famine-hit areas. Both railways were built by far-sighted Maharajahs. The Darjeeling Himalayan Railway – the world's first mountain railway – of course carried the world-famous Darjeeling tea. The Kalka-Shimla mountain railway bore the Viceroy to his summer capital, the remote hill-station from where he ruled his vast empire. The prospects for the survival of these mountain railways have been enhanced by UNESCO which has granted them World Heritage status. But it's greatly to the credit of Indian Railways that they showed no sign of closing them, even though they no longer serve their original purposes.

So how can we argue that the railways Angus travelled should survive when they were

Left: Kangra Valley Railway, Kangra, 16 April 2007

INTRODUCTION

Six of us spilled out of the carriage into the sunlight, crossing a blinding piece of tarmac to the station building. Behind pink walls and blue doors, everything was locked except the first class waiting room. A handful of antique chairs, clustered about a heavy round table, filled the space. Nobody sat down.

The Divisional Manager, the Senior Commercial Manager and the Senior Divisional Engineer paused politely before making their goodbyes. Then they scrambled to the waiting cars. Between them they ran Baroda Division of the Indian Railways, pushing 400 trains a day through a city of four million, including a section of the main Bombay-Delhi line.[1] This was not that line.

The Assistant Divisional Engineer, the Assistant Running Manager and I poked about the station. There was an old set of scales, a ticket window and a parcel room. In the station master's office a desk, a wooden cabinet, a drooping calendar and a phone were just visible through the glazed door, all covered in a thick layer of dust. Across the street, the buildings of the railway colony formed a line of low blocks parallel to the station. Half a dozen loafers lounged in the shade of the waiting area, but out in the sun, nothing moved. "This colony is gradually being abandoned," said the Assistant Divisional Engineer with a touch of melancholy. "Already the medical centre has been closed."

Across the platform, the locomotive hissed and throbbed, impatient for the return run. Heat and diesel fumes rose from its battered panels and vented hoods as it lumbered like a buffalo into its shunt. With a series of back and forth movements, it swapped positions with the observation car that had brought us to Jambusar. On the return run to Baroda, we would be travelling backwards.

The observation deck had windows at the back and sides, giving a panoramic view from the rear of the train. Inside were wood panelled walls and floral curtains, and a white tablecloth laden with bowls of sweets and bottles of mineral water. It can't have been too different from the way the Baroda royal family travelled, in the days when the line belonged to them. A private sleeping compartment lay just behind the observation deck, and a galley and servants' quarters took up the rear. Kitchen staff kept up a nonstop supply of tea, biscuits, sandwiches, soft drinks, chips, cashew nuts and cake.

The train ambled through fallow fields as we began the return run. A large industrial plant was visible in the hazy distance, followed by one or two other factories that loomed and vanished above the straggling countryside. Even in this forgotten corner, the brave new India of enterprise and industry squatted on the horizon.

A few hours earlier, over the first round of tea and Britannia butter cookies, Mr Srivastava, the Divisional Manager, had opened his briefcase and pulled out a sheaf of photocopies, maps and spiral bound reports. Poring over a colour coded map of the Baroda railways, we had followed a trail of blue hatched lines with our fingers: the local narrow gauge network. Or what was left of it. Mr Srivastava, who spoke of railway heritage the way others talk of cricket, liked to refer to the division's 600 kilometres of narrow gauge, but this is the historical figure. Today, there are about 300 kilometres still in operation. We were on one of those lines, the track spinning gently out below the little train as the cotton fields slipped by.

"This was a very remote area," said Mr Srivastava, a talkative man with a cherub face and a silvering thatch of hair. "The rulers of Baroda were quite progressive. They wanted to connect the people of these districts to Baroda. They used narrow gauge because it was more affordable."

Now the two feet six inches (762 milimetres) line was under survey for conversion to broad gauge, which in India means five feet six inches (1676 milimetres). Assets would be measured, quantities assessed, strengths tested, and costs and benefits compared. But for now, the narrow gauge line was barely bothering to compete with the roads. Most of its stations were unstaffed, with the passengers buying their tickets from the guard. A track maintenance unit had been shifted from Jambusar to Baroda six months ago, reducing the staff at the station from a hundred to twenty.

Just one train a day ran along the line, departing Baroda at 10.00am. The day we caught it, it completed the return journey at 6.00pm – eight hours to cover 122 kilometres. A travelling gateman operated the level crossings, climbing down to close the gates, then clambering back on board once the train had crossed. The line was

Left: Barak Valley Express, 25 February 2007

---

1. Because the text of this book deals with both the past and the present, for consistency the older renderings of place names have been used.

Above: Kangra Valley Railway, Pathankot, 6 April 2011

half its original length, as one section had been closed and another converted to broad gauge, serving a port and a chemical complex. The narrow gauge lines were not economical any more, requiring constant maintenance with scarce equipment, with no freight business to bring a return. On the Jambusar branch, villagers were only taking the train because it was cheaper than the road service.

We pulled through station after abandoned station – Ankhi, Masar Road, Mobharda – sturdy structures finished in faded pink or yellow distemper, with tiny ticket windows and waiting areas shaded by swooping corrugated roofs. At each stop a small knot of people would step on or off the train. There were perhaps 50 on board at any one time.

I had fetched up in Baroda two days before knowing only that, after riding narrow and metre gauge trains in the farthest corners of India, this was where the story began. Not in Baroda exactly, but in nearby Dabhoi, a 1500-year-old trading town now languishing in dusty obscurity. But it had had its moments of glory. In 1862, when the American Civil War caused a worldwide shortage of cotton, Dabhoi caught a commercial wave when it became the terminus of India's first narrow gauge railway. The 32 kilometre track linked the rich cotton growing district to the new broad gauge line at Miyagam, giving access to Bombay and the world.

Nowadays Dabhoi looked a bit down on its luck: a few finely carved old houses and a grubby bazaar where hawkers croaked from behind piles of dates, popcorn, and shell-shaped sugar cakes. In place of the weaving and metalwork for which the town had once been known, shops sold saris of sequined chiffon, and steel almirahs in lurid greens and purples. Dabhoi's most famous feature, its thirteenth century carved gates, were impressive but a little neglected.

"This was the busiest narrow gauge junction in the world," Mr Srivastava told me the afternoon that I met him in his airy 1920s office. Expecting 20 minutes of the DRM's time, I got two hours.

"At the time it was built there was no model for narrow gauge in India. It had never been done. So they had to work things out by experimentation." Eager to open up the rich hinterland, the Gaekwad ("protector of cows", or maharaja) of Baroda decided on rail because the roads became impassable in the rains. Three steam engines were imported, but the original line, built with thirteen-pounds-per-yard rails, was not strong enough to support them. So for the first 11 years the trains were drawn by bullocks.

"It was converted to steam in 1873. The British had suggested 55 pound rails, which they would supply – all the equipment came from Britain at that time. But the Gaekwad worked out that 30 pounds would be sufficient. After this, many more extensions were built. If you look at the financial records you will see that it was a great success. They even took over a British line, to the port of Dahej, and made it profitable."

This was interesting. India's narrow gauge railways, so often associated with the British and their hill stations, were actually a local innovation, sponsored by a raja with more on his mind than dancing girls and precious stones. India's first narrow gauge network was built, not to help colonials escape the heat, but as a hard headed investment in the future. The Illustrated London News approved. "A native prince has at last constructed a railway at his own cost, and has thus, we may hope, inaugurated the investment of native capital in great public works," its correspondent exulted, even if his impatience was a little uncalled for – the pioneering Ffestiniog narrow gauge railway in Wales only began to use steam in 1863.

Eventually five lines ran from Dabhoi, including a connection to Baroda. Cotton, grain and mogra – jasmine flowers – were the main cargo, but there were other incentives.

An extension was built to Bhadarpur to fetch stone for the Gaekwad's palace, and another to the Narmada River at Chandod, a pilgrimage site. But the railway was just one innovation among many. Sayajirao Gaekwad, who ruled from 1875 to 1939, introduced universal free primary education, founded worthy institutions including a bank and a library, and gave jobs to national leaders including Dadabhai Naoroji and Dr Ambedkar. If Dabhoi today is a backwater, Baroda is one of India's most important centres of finance and industry.

Construction continued until 1919, with a web of lines connecting to river traffic on the Narmada, and others reaching into remote and tribal areas. "The tribal people at this time began to incorporate the trains into their paintings, which are called pithora," said Mr Srivastava. "We have even commissioned one for our museum." The line from Pratapnagar to Jambusar was one of the last to be completed.

That line continued to pay out beneath the observation car, the sleepers poking like dinosaur bones from the eroding sides of the narrow embankment. More biscuits and bottles of water appeared from the galley, but by now we were slouching in our cane chairs as the sun pushed relentlessly through the floral curtains. Outside were mango and lemon orchards, and fields of marigolds and tobacco. Camels were tethered beside huts, and grey skinned bullocks ploughed in pairs. We arrived at Padra, where the ghost of a double track appeared briefly. This had been the terminus before the line was extended to Jambusar, and just as 100 years ago the network had been expanding steadily, it now seemed to be receding before our eyes.

By 2008 two of the narrow gauge lines radiating from Dabhoi had been converted to broad gauge, while another had been closed. Of the two that remained, one was a once-daily service to Chandod that left Dabhoi at 8.00am, arrived at about nine, and turned around almost immediately. The day I took it, the passengers consisted of a couple of farmers and a prosperous Baroda family on an outing. Chandod was another slice of age-old India, a tranquil street of neoclassical facades ending at the tourquoise sheen of the Narmada, where shaven headed pilgrims washed away their sins.

The oldest length of narrow gauge on the subcontinent was a bit busier. Three trains a day ran on the line from Dabhoi to Miyagam, lazily collecting a more or less full load of commuters and villagers from tumbledown stations, and dropping them in town for work or shopping. The fields on either side of the line are still thick with cotton, but these days the crop moves by truck.

Narrow and metre gauge railways are gradually becoming extinct all over India, but in booming, bankable Baroda, they were literally being turned into a museum exhibit. Mr Srivastava had established a museum and heritage park at Pratapnagar – the narrow gauge station in Baroda – just two months earlier, and another heritage park at Dabhoi. Ironically, the line that connects the two stations was converted to broad gauge in 2008. Every morning and evening it moves thousands of commuters – students, office workers – in and out of the bustling hub of Baroda in a way that a narrow gauge service could never manage.

Above: Kangra Valley Railway, Jawalamukhi Marg, 16 April 2007
Left: Kalka-Shimla Railway, Dharampur, 8 March 2007

Left: Gwalior Light Railway, Bamour Gaon, 8 March 2011
Right: Dabhoi Railways, Chandod (top) and Kayavardhan (bottom), 15 March 2011

This book was compiled from travels on narrow and metre gauge lines all over India, recording a way of life that is drawing to a close. Of the 11 lines that appear here, only four have an assured future. Those are the Kalka-Shimla Railway, the Matheran Light Railway and the Nilgiri Mountain railway, all of which serve popular tourist routes. The Darjeeling Himalayan Railway still caters to tourists and locals, but is in a poor state of repair.

The government of India has committed to converting all except these mountain railways to broad gauge, in the interest of improved services and easier transhipment. The conversion of Assam's Barak Valley Railway from metre gauge is already underway, and presumably the various metre gauge lines traversing Rajasthan's Aravali plateau will follow. Much of the two feet six inches Satpura network[2] in central India has already been converted, while the Shakuntala Express, a single line of the same gauge serving a number of small communities in Maharashtra, is hanging on by the skin of its teeth. The two feet (610 milimetres) gauge Gwalior Light Railway is under consideration for conversion, and there are persistent calls to convert the two feet six inches Kangra Valley Railway.

My travels to document these railways began in Kangra, when I decided to take a ride on one of India's lesser known mountain trains. I had lived in the area for some time by then, but the route taken by the railway opened up forest groves and plunging gorges and glistening mountain views that I had never guessed at. Kangra is one of the most beautiful – and underrated – corners of the Himalayas, and the line hugged its contours as if by nature. I was hooked. I rode the rails for a week taking photographs, and then moved on to other hill trains – the Kalka-Shimla, the Darjeeling Himalayan and the Nilgiri Mountain Railway.

Each of these is a spectacular example of ingenuity in a gorgeous landscape, and highly photogenic, but they are also well-known tourist routes. Not that there is anything artificial about this – one of the reasons these railways were built was to carry crowds of holidaymakers, and the fact that they are doing exactly that over 100 years later is an astonishing feat of maintenance and preservation. In this sense the mountain railways are not so much museum pieces as living treasures. But as I explored life on other, local lines, which have served communities for between half and one and a half centuries, I became aware that I was witnessing a way of life that was on the verge of disappearing. It seemed worthwhile to attempt to document that life.

The project broadened to include more obscure lines, services that had already enjoyed an extended lifespan. These were trains that had survived so far because they did a job of work. In Maharashtra and Gujarat, the Shakuntala and Dabhoi lines, built to haul cotton, had continued to operate as passenger transport. Assam's Barak Valley line, its freight business long ago decimated by Partition, still carried a heavy load of humanity through hypnotic hills feathered with bamboo and haunted by insurgents. Beneath palace ramparts in the storybook cities of Gwalior and Udaipur, railways built by benevolent princes laboured on into the twenty-first century, kept from retirement by the sheer weight of demand.

Many of these railways had local origins. The Matheran Light Railway was the lifetime obsession of a Parsee entrepreneur from Bombay. The Gwalior, Aravali and Dabhoi lines were constructed by the rulers of princely states, part social service and part status symbol. Others were privately owned, appealing to investors because they were cheap to build and operate. Encouraged by tax incentives from a government daunted by the task of connecting every part of India by rail, narrow and metre gauge lines were built as feeder routes connecting suppliers to markets. Some were built as famine relief, while

half a dozen of them serviced those quintessentially Indian industries – tea and cotton. While the colonial government used narrow gauge mostly to conquer the Himalayas, the indigenous lines spawned tales of rulers who outwitted or snubbed the British, while borrowing their technology to develop and strengthen their domains.

The lines that exist today are the remnants of a network that once covered much of India. Metre gauge at its peak boasted 25,000 kilometres of track, now down to about 9,000. Following the example of the Gaekwads of Baroda, half a dozen or so rulers of princely states built narrow or metre gauge railways, while British companies established others. The largest narrow gauge network was the Satpura, originally part of the Bengal Nagpur Railway, with over 1000 kilometres of track.

Most of these lines have now been closed or converted, but the handful that remain mean that India is essentially the only country in the world with a working narrow gauge system, as opposed to lines that operate for the tourist trade. It is a remarkable survival, but not surprising in a country which finds its identity in diversity, and where threads of ancient tradition weave through the fabric of everyday existence. These little trains are so much a part of Indian life that it is difficult to imagine the country without them. They are testament to India's ability to absorb outside influences, to adapt them and ultimately incorporate them into its own being. In this they symbolise perhaps the greatest genius of Indian culture.

And they epitomise the breadth and depth of India. The trains run through mountains, deserts, steamy tea gardens and shivering fields of wheat. They carry farmers, holy men and the destitute, as well as well heeled holidaymakers escaping frenetic cities. Animals are everywhere, on the lines, at the stations and sometimes even on board the trains – cows, goats, sheep, monkeys, dogs, buffalo, chickens, peacocks, deer, neelgai, even the occasional elephant. If there is a microcosm of Indian life in all its variety and fecundity, its pathos and its grace, its strangeness and its beauty, these trains are likely to be it.

Throughout these journeys, and some of them were miserable, day-long affairs in carriages so crowded you could barely breathe, there was always great good humour. No matter how broken down the train, how paltry the food, how hot (or cold) the day, how comfortless or collapsed the stations, people seemed to approach the journey with a sense of adventure and companionship. There was always a laugh to be had, and the more outrageous the situation, the funnier people seemed to find it. Prostrating yourself on the roof of a carriage to dodge the girders of a bridge because otherwise they would take your head off? Hilarious.

The most amusing thing of all was to have a foreigner on board. Poking an outsized camera into the lives of strangers isn't regarded with favour in every culture, but I was never made to feel less than completely welcome, and more often treated as an honoured guest. The trust, the openness and the humour were identical in Rajasthan, Assam, Himachal Pradesh, Punjab, Haryana, West Bengal, Madhya Pradesh, Tamil Nadu, Gujarat and Maharashtra. If this shows through in the photos, then I've succeeded in what I set out to do.

The staff of the railways were just as welcoming. In many cases they are using equipment that is a hundred or more years old to run services essential to thousands of people, through rugged mountains, parched deserts, monsoon downpours or sliding hillsides. Much of the time the trains run like clockwork, and when that doesn't happen, you still know one will turn up eventually. The staff of all these railways do a wonderful job, with dedication and ingenuity. Most of all they take pride, a pride that was palpable as I was shown over workshops and stations, signal systems and locomotives. The

2. This system, based around Nagpur, has not been given its own chapter.

survival of the narrow and metre gauge railways exemplifies an ability to extract every ounce of value from a resource – a talent likely to be even more important in this century than it was in the last.

There is also a strong consciousness of heritage. The Darjeeling, Kalka-Shimla, Nilgiri and Kangra Valley railways have been accorded World Heritage status, while the museum and heritage parks at Pratapnagar and Dabhoi are wonderful facilities. There are railway museums in Delhi, Calcutta, Nagpur, Tinsukia and Kurseong. The Kalka-Shimla, Matheran, Kangra and Nilgiri railways are in exceptional condition, and there is no doubt that enough tangible reminders of the narrow gauge era will survive for future generations to enjoy. But my interest in these railways is not so much in their physical structures, as in the life that surrounds them. Born of the intimacy of tiny carriages, a sense of locality, and a slower pace, the texture of that life is one of simplicity and humanity. These characteristics make it all the more worth recording.

-×-

The train had entered the outskirts of Baroda, passing furniture shops and hardware stores, and walls plastered with advertisements for home appliances. On the other side of the track, new residences glowed white in the sun beside the concrete frames of fast rising apartment blocks. "Labh Residency – all modern amenities. The essence of spirituality", read one billboard. "Imperial Heights – futuristic business spaces", said another. We passed through a short tunnel and arrived at Vishvamitri station, where a banyan tree shed its shade on some sleeping dogs. Just behind, the line to Delhi vaulted the narrow gauge track at right angles. A few minutes later we passed the remnant of the Gaekwad's personal station, an abandoned platform adjacent to the palace grounds, and a few minutes after that we pulled into Pratapnagar, where the blue-on-blue coaches of the new broad gauge train to Dabhoi stood waiting. Stepping down from the observation car, I thanked to the Assistant Divisional Engineer and the Assistant Running Manager, crossed the tracks and joined the bigger train to a chorus of "Hello!" and "Which country?"

A week or so before, while squeezed tight inside an overcrowded carriage on the Gwalior Light Railway, a farmer had leaned across and asked me when the bara train would come. He wanted to know when the line would be converted to broad gauge. At the time of writing no decision had been taken, but I could see his point. To do the full 200 kilometre run from Gwalior to Sheopur Kalan takes at least ten hours, and the time I did it, the carriage was so packed I was not able to leave my seat the entire time. Hundreds more travelled on the roof.

There is no point being sentimental about the passing of some of these lines. Riding the roof of an ancient train through a classical landscape is a romantic experience once or twice in a lifetime, but for the 15,000 souls who ride the Gwalior line every day, conversion to broad gauge would deliver dramatic improvements in safety, speed and comfort. The conversion of the Barak Valley track will hopefully bring a much improved service to a neglected part of India. What remains of the Satpura network is also overcrowded and ripe for conversion, while the Shakuntala Express has little of its original character left to preserve, with most of the stations long abandoned. If conversion encourages passengers to stick with rail instead of adding their numbers to already crowded roads, all the better. Overcrowding is far from being a problem on the two narrow gauge lines that still run from Dabhoi, and these might well survive because of their historical importance. And it would be lovely to see the Darjeeling Himalayan Railway restored to its original glory.

Above: Aravali Railways, Dungarpur, 25 March 2011

That leaves the Kangra Valley Railway, which seems just fine the way it is. The line carries relatively few passengers, especially in its upper reaches, and mostly bypasses the big towns. There seems no need for an expanded service, and conversion would alter the character of the line forever, including reconstruction of two of the most attractive rail bridges in India – the bridges over Reond Khad and Bathu Khad. Laid down in the late 1920s, the Kangra railway is one of the last of its breed – a local narrow gauge railway in original working order. It probably has a few decades left in it before it needs to be upgraded, closed, or turned into a tourist attraction. Let it run.

I had one more meeting with Mr Srivastava before I left Baroda. He had already arranged the trip to Jambusar, and a guided tour of the museum and heritage parks, and I had become used to his kindness and his enthusiasm. But this time I sat in as he knocked heads together to get the Baroda suburban trains running on time, then entertained a team from the construction division. The subject of broad gauge conversion came up, and Mr Srivastava waxed lyrical again – not about the value of narrow gauge, but about the benefits of converting it. The broad gauge lines were reaching out to the backward areas. They were helping to develop tourism. Rail enthusiasts would flock to Dabhoi. The upgraded line to Chhota Udaipur gave access to the Sardar Sarovar reservoir on the Narmada, with its parks and its wildlife. The converted line to Dahej connected the port to the rest of the network. Conversion of the Gwalior line would open up a new, shorter route to the coast.

Then before we noticed, Mr Srivastava had segued into the history of the Gwalior Light Railway. His last posting had been in Gwalior. Now, that had been an interesting time.

Right: Dabhoi Railways, Ganpatpura and Kural, 15 March 2011

THE GWALIOR LIGHT RAILWAY

THE GWALIOR LIGHT RAILWAY

Gauge: Two feet
Length: 200 kilometres
Location: Madhya Pradesh
Route: Gwalior to Sheopur Kalan via Sabalgarh
Year of completion: 1909

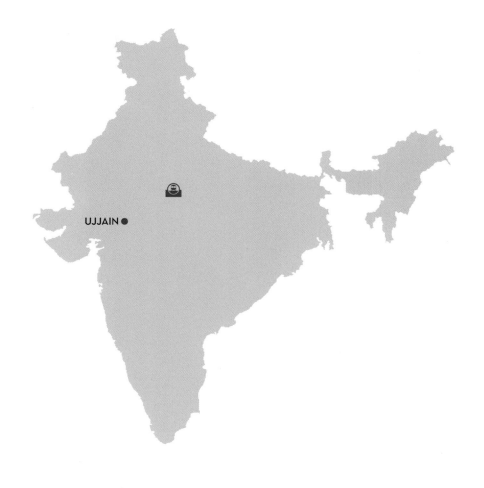

UJJAIN ●

In *Princess: The Autobiography of the Dowager Maharani of Gwalior*, the author tells a cute story about her father-in-law's childhood. In the 1880s Madhavrao Scindia, who became Maharaja of Gwalior while still a boy, had a British tutor called Mr Johnstone. When Mr Johnstone went on leave to England, the prince asked him to bring back a toy train. But the railway that Mr Johnstone brought back was more than a toy. It was half a mile of two foot gauge line, complete with engine and carriages. The prince had the line installed inside the palace, but there was not enough track to run the train properly. So another two miles were ordered, taking the rails as far as Morar, in the city. A year or so later, the line was extended to Sussera, where the royal family liked to shoot.

The Gwalior Light Railway might have begun life as a royal toy, but Madhavrao was still a young ruler when it took on a serious purpose. By the 1890s famine was threatening the state, and the maharaja ordered the line be extended to the towns of Sipri and Bhind as part of a relief scheme. Both branches opened in 1899. The choice of two foot gauge – the narrowest in India, and otherwise only used in the mountains – originated with the toy railway, and possibly a certain amount of anti-imperial stubbornness. The British suggested two and a half feet because it was more suitable for military use, but the Maharaja refused, citing the difficulty of building the

wider gauge in the ravine country around Gwalior. The state had been building railways in partnership with the central government for over 20 years, and may have felt it had been getting a raw deal.

Madhavrao believed in railways as key to the development of the drought prone state. A further branch of the network was built to Sheopur Kalan, a remote area that these days is intensely irrigated and farmed with mustard, chickpeas and wheat. The farmlands alternate with wildernesses of gnarled acacia, where deer, peacocks and neelgai roam free. The line was built in four stages between 1904 and 1909. A line from Ujjain to Agar, two cities far to the southwest of Gwalior, was opened in 1932. Gwalior also had a circular suburban line. The Maharaja himself used the railways to travel to his hunting lodge at Sipri (now Shivpuri), and to the horse races at Gola ka Mandir. The only branch of the line that is still narrow gauge is the Gwalior to Sheopur Kalan section. The suburban line is closed, and the lines to Shivpuri and Bhind have been converted to broad gauge. The railway at Ujjain closed in the 1970s. There is no line leading out of the fort these days, but the existing track skirts beneath its imposing walls, cutting through the city and passing within feet of people's porches as it begins its run to Sabalgarh and Sheopur Kalan.

Page 25: Driver en route to Tarrakalan from Silipur, 9 March 2011
Above: Gwalior, 8 March 2011

Above: Tarrakalan, 11 March 2011
Right: Bamour Gaon, 9 March 2011

Left: Namkeen hawker, Motijheel to Milaoli,
8 March 2011

Right: Sumaoli, 9 March 2011

Left: Napping on the roof, Sumaoli to Thara, 9 March 2011

Right: Sikroda, 11 March 2011

Page 32–3: Bamour Gaon to Ambikeshwar,
8 March 2011

Left: Sabalgarh, 10 March 2011
Above: Beneath Sabalgarh Fort, 10 March 2011

Above: Jora Alapur, 8 March 2011

" The train has barely left Gwalior before it plunges into an undulating desert of twisted acacia populated by deer, nilgai and peacocks. Just as suddenly it slips back into a rural idyll. Fields of wheat, chickpeas and mustard, irrigated by pump-houses with the look of medieval granaries, are fringed by feathery lines of trees softening the horizon. All the elements of bucolic classicism are there: the wicker gate, the buffalo lined up companionably in their stalls, the hand-pump, the threshing yard. Pats of cow dung bearing hand prints are piled into worshipful mounds, shaped like hayricks or temples. Now, the terrain alternates between eerie scrubland and bountiful farms. The skirts and cholis and the turbans and dhotis of rural Madhya Pradesh start to appear. For the last few hours of the journey the train crosses a series of dry canals, broken ravines and a deep, green river which echoes back the hollow thunder from the steel bridge. "

Left: Gwalior, 12 March 2011
Right: Gwalior, 8 March 2011

THE DARJEELING
HIMALAYAN RAILWAY

THE DARJEELING HIMALAYAN RAILWAY

CALCUTTA ●

Gauge: Two feet
Length: 88 kilometres
Location: West Bengal
Route: New Jalpaiguri to Darjeeling
Elevation: 122-2225 metres
Year of completion: 1881

The most famous mountain railway in India is also the oldest. The line was built to connect the unrivalled tea growing district of Darjeeling to Calcutta via the terminus at Siliguri, which had been completed in 1878. Travelling to the hill station at the time involved taking a tonga up Hill Cart Road, a slow and somewhat nerve wracking journey skirting sharp curves and plunging mountainsides. When the railway was built it largely followed the road, crossing it repeatedly and cutting along the main streets of towns along the way. The steep gradient was overcome with a couple of ingenious innovations. One of these was the installation of reversing stations, where the train would back up through a Z-shaped section of track to gain height before moving forward again. The other was the use of loops, where the line would circle over itself in a tight curve. These were modified repeatedly over the years, following landslides or simply to improve the performance of the line, starting after the inaugural run, when several trains derailed. The line currently incorporates six reverses and three loops.

With the improved connection, Darjeeling became a popular hill station, and by 1909–10 the train was carrying 174,000 passengers a year. At the top, if a traveller is lucky they might catch a glimpse of India's highest mountain, Kanchenjunga,

8586 metres, whose five summits dwarf the town. Cloud and mist are so predominant in Darjeeling that a sighting of the sacred mountain is believed to be a blessing from the gods. With its cool climate the area became a centre for school education, and remains so today. Ghum station, at 2225 metres, is the highest in India. Branches were added from Siliguri to Kishanganj in 1914 and Siliguri to Kalimpong in 1915.

The Darjeeling Himalayan Railway has had a turbulent history, surviving two earthquakes and numerous landslides. Politics has also played a role, with the line forming a vital link between depots during the Second World War, and ferrying wounded soldiers to convalesce in the hills. Partition in 1947 meant that Assam was cut off from the rest of India except for a 20 kilometre wide corridor through West Bengal, with much of the broad gauge network ceded to East Pakistan. This left no rail link to the northeastern states, and the Kishanganj branch of the DHR as the only connection to the now crucial staging point of Siliguri. The whole network was acquired by the government of India in 1948 so it could convert the Kishanganj line to metre gauge as part of the remarkable Assam Rail Link Project, which forged a metre gauge system across the rugged base of the Himalayas to reconnect the northeast by 1950. The Kalimpong branch was closed

in 1950, and the Darjeeling line was extended to meet the broad gauge network at New Jalpaiguri in 1962. The line was closed for 18 months in 1988–9 during the agitation for an independent Gorkhaland. The Darjeeling Himalayan Railway was the first Indian railway to be placed on the UNESCO World Heritage list in 1999, the second railway in the world to receive this recognition.

Gandhi travelled on the line, as did Mark Twain. The Albanian nun Agnes Gonxha Bojaxhiu, later known more recognisably as Mother Teresa, had a visitation telling her to work with the homeless of Calcutta while riding the train in 1946. The occultist Aleister Crowley, travelling in 1905, was impressed both by the changing scenery and the ability of his female porter to carry his wardrobe trunk unaided, weighed down as it was with axes, rifles, revolvers, scientific instruments and books. Twain thought the journey was "the most enjoyable day I have spent on earth".

Page 42–3: Locomotive shed, Darjeeling, 4 April 2007
Above: Loop Four, "Agony Point", 4 April 2007

Left: Sukna, 2 April 2007

Right, clockwise from top left: Darjeeling, Kurseong to Tung,
approaching Batasia Loop, Siliguri to Sukna, April 2007

Left & right: Kurseong bazaar, 4 April 2007

Above: Sonada bazaar, 4 April 2007
Right: Darjeeling, 2 April 200

> Tea-pickers with baskets walk along the track in gumboots. I look back towards Tung and see the line of settlements that follows the tracks, forest-green houses with tin eaves and tiny balconies decorated with pansies. There is a growing air of calm as we ascend despite the dramatic vertical valley. Terraces peek out from the haze, and we drive straight through the bazaar at Sonada. The valley is a mass of grey now, the only colour the primary hues of prayer flags strung around a white stupa. The train's fog lights have been switched on, and passengers break out their sweaters. We pass the ropeway in the midst of pine groves, but at Jor Bungalow all is again lost in the darkening mist. At almost half past six in the evening excited voices begin to call out 'Darjeeling!', the town itself identified by pinpricks of light in an indigo gloaming. With jerking progress we nose our way slowly past hair salons and chicken shops and tin trunk sellers, and we have arrived.

Above: Kurseong, 4 April 2007
Opposite: Tindharia sidings, 2 April 2007

"" At the first loop – between Mahananda and Rang Tong – the forest becomes denser, jungle-like, less formed. The ridge opposite is swathed in haze. We make brisk progress to our first reverse when the word 'Backside!' is shouted out by the guard and the word reverberates around the carriage, and families stifle giggles. The reverse takes three minutes, then on we move past tiny blue-painted wood huts with tin shoulders perched on the hillside below us. ""

Page 54–5: Rang Tong, 4 April 2007
Top Left: Kurseong, 4 April 2007
Bottom Left: Darjeeling, 2 April 2007
Right: Sukna, 2 April 2007

Above: Darjeeling, 2 April 2007

Page 58–9: Tindharia sidings, 2 April 2007

Page 59, top: Locomotive 779 "Himalayan Bird", Darjeeling, 4 April 2007

Page 59, top: Boilerplate, Darjeeling, 4 April 2007

Above: Darjeeling, 4 April 2007
Right: Kanchenjunga from Darjeeling, 4 April 2007

"Before the fourth reverse the valley opens onto terraces below, and the cool air starts to caress. Steep forested hills, dotted with houses, fall away, and we pass chortens and bright prayer flags. The ridge-tops are lost in clouds and, at the reverse, locals begin to hop on for the short run up the hill to Darjeeling. Tracks cling to the mountain edges and the horn blows, like a mournful trumpet."

THE BARAK VALLEY EXPRESS

THE BARAK
VALLEY EXPRESS

Gauge: Metre
Length: 215 kilometres
Location: Assam
Route: Lumding to Silchar via Badarpur
Year of completion: 1904

CALCUTTA ●

● CHITTAGONG

The Barak Valley line was part of a larger network built to connect the highly productive industries of Assam and eastern Bengal to the newly developed port of Chittagong, in an effort to avoid transport bottlenecks around Calcutta. The Assam Bengal Railway Company was formed in 1892 to build the line, with the Chittagong-Cachar section through the plains completed in 1898, and the remainder by 1904. The section through the mountainous area between Silchar, the capital of Cachar, and Lumding, on the main line to Guwahati, presented challenges to construction including heavy rainfall, landslides, mosquitoes, rugged terrain and a shortage of labour and material. "It is said by travellers who have seen the mountain sections of other railways in India, and in other parts of the world, that the engineering difficulties met with in the North Cachar Hills are equal to any of them and that the scenery is unsurpassed," quoted imperial compiler Somerset Playne in his book *Bengal and Assam, Behar and Orissa: Their History, People, Commerce and Industrial Resources.*

The completed line was a success. Writing in 1917, Playne listed 110 locomotives, numerous coal trucks and 3,000 covered goods wagons bringing tea and jute to the busy port, and transporting imported salt, oil, tea machinery and corrugated iron back up the line. The passenger service was also impressive, Playne noted, its forty-three-foot coaches "furnished and fitted in an up-to-date style and lighted with Pintsch's patent

gas apparatus." During the Second World War, the merged and renamed Bengal Assam Railway assumed strategic importance when Japan attempted to invade India through Nagaland. The Battle of Kohima in 1944, when an outnumbered garrison prevented the Japanese army from gaining access to the railhead at Dimapur, was one of the decisive actions of the war and the beginning of the Japanese retreat from mainland Asia.

The Partition of India in 1947 was a devastating setback for the Assam railways. With the creation of East Pakistan and its hastily drawn boundaries, the northeastern states were all but cut off from the rest of India, with the only access a twenty kilometre wide corridor in West Bengal. The rail links to Assam were severed with the cession of a large part of the network to Pakistan, replaced with a hastily constructed metre gauge section in 1950. Assam also lost its direct connection to the coast, with Chittagong falling on the Pakistan side of the border. The Barak Valley railway fell into obscurity, suffering poor maintenance and a loss of freight traffic because of its remoteness. Security has been another issue, with insurgent groups occasionally attacking the line. Conversion to broad gauge began in 1998, but has proved as problematic as the original construction, with the upgrade still not completed at the time of writing.

Page 62–3: Bardarpur Junction, 20 February 2007
Above: "Rhinoceros unicornis", indigenous to Assam,
on an engine at Harangajao, 18 February 2007

Above: Lumding Junction, 25 February 2007

Right: Military train, Katakhal Junction, 17 February 2007

“ The Barak Valley Railway is itself a reminder of that wrenching episode: the creation of East Pakistan. Running down a slender corridor on the far side of Bangladesh, the line was built to connect the tea gardens of Assam to the port of Chittagong, and opened in 1903. But the link to the sea was cut by partition and the railway dangles like a fraying rope, tenuously linking this remote corner of Assam to the rest of India. Jobs are short in India's Northeast. Immigrants from Bangladesh and other parts of India add to the volatile mix of local animist, Christian and Hindu tribes, and violence explodes from time to time. Every passenger train on this line has a carriage designated 'Military'. ”

Left: Kalachand to Maibang,
25 February 2007

Right; top: Weighing scales and biscuit
jars at Silchar Junction; bottom: Mahur to
Migrendisa, 20 February 2007

Next to me, a man is calmly reading a Bible in English. When he's done, I introduce myself. 'S.N. Rao', he says. He's from Hyderabad, in South India. He is a government headmaster, posted to a school in Tinsukia district, upper Assam. He's travelling to Silchar to attend a conference. He will stay for a day, then return the way he came, a 20 hour journey. One way. When he goes back to Hyderabad, once or twice a year, it takes him three days.

"Snack vendors work their way up and down the train, wriggling and side-stepping their way through the crowd, stopping to create elaborate concoctions from their compartmented trays. One snack is called channa – chickpeas mixed with puffed rice, onions, coriander, lemon, oil, chilli and chutney, and shaken vigorously in a well used plastic jar. It tastes of horseradish. Another one is called jal muri, of fried gram flour and puffed rice. Cashews, peanuts and glacé cherries are extra."

Left: Channa masala, Ditokcherra,
25 February 2007
Above: Ditokcherra, 25 February 2007

Above: Badarpur Junction, 20 February 2007
Right: Haflong Hill, 17 February 2007

 Just as I'm thinking nothing is going to happen the whole day, something, inevitably, does. A group of young tribal people has clambered on board in one large mass. One is wearing a t-shirt that reads 'Brat Bravery'. Another's says 'God's Girl'. They look as if they might have come from a rock concert, but they're on their way home from a Christian youth conference. They are from the Hmar tribe. By the time we reach Haflong Hill, the highest point of the route and a kind of apotheosis, they have begun to sing. It starts with Brat Bravery and her friend. They are joined by a few more, and more still, until about twenty voices swell to fill the carriage, almost drowning the clack-clack of the wheels. I don't understand the words or recognise the tunes, but the songs have an ache to them, like an old black American hymn. And the voices have a power which seems to rise from that ache, and finally overcome it, at least for as long as the song lasts. They sing with narrowed eyes and contorted faces, tears streaming. One song lasts about 15 minutes, its chorus an intense, repeating cadence which gathers power like a steam engine pulling out of a station, finally achieving a rhythm which pounds with a beautiful intensity. By the end of it, every singer is in tears, enraptured. A few more songs follow, lighter and shorter. One of them sounds a little like 'Amazing Grace'. The journey is no longer enervating.

Above: Haflong Hill, the highest point of the line, 17 February 2007
Left: Siesta at Harangajao, 18 February 2007

THE ARAVALI RAILWAYS

THE ARAVALI RAILWAYS

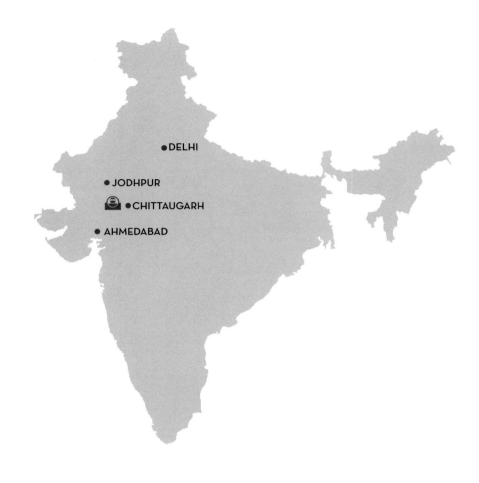

Gauge: Metre
Length: Mavli-Marwar 152 kilometres,
Udaipur-Dungarpur 105 kilometres
Location: Rajasthan
Route: Lumding to Silchar via Badarpur
Year of completion: Mavli-Marwar 1936,
Udaipur-Dungarpur 1960s

According to a story told in Udaipur, Queen Victoria once asked for a map of the princely state of Mewar. The ruler, suspecting her motives, sent her a papad, and the British took the hint – they never annexed the state. Mewar sits on Rajasthan's rough, dry, orange-soiled Aravali plateau, and its rulers, known as maharanas, long treasured their independence. Local mythology tells of a god called Srinathji, an avatar of Krishna, who was invited by the Maharana to visit the city but could not reach it in the prescribed period of one night. He remains to this day at the temple of Nathdwara, 40 kilometres away. Another legend tells how the first maharana, Bapa Rawal, was condemned by his guru only to rule the place where he stood.

Mewar is harsh, impenetrable country, but at its centre, like a jewel, lies the old capital, Udaipur. Ringed by hills and studded with carved havelis, the city straddles a lake where pleasure gardens nestle on small islands. Resplendent above it all is the palace of the maharanas, who held out against both the Mughals and the British. Fateh Singh, said to be seventy-third in the royal line, built schools, hospitals, a college and, in 1896, a metre gauge railway that connected to the Delhi line at Chittor (now Chittaurgarh), the one-time Mewar capital sacked by the Mughal emperor Akbar. He

took the train to Delhi to meet the viceroy, Lord Curzon, at the Delhi Durbar in 1903, but returned without getting off the train when he discovered that he had been ranked below the rulers of five other states. He refused to attend the Durbar in 1911 with George V, and ten years later would not receive the Prince of Wales at Udaipur. Not long after this he was deposed in favour of his son, Bhupal Singh.

Almost half a century later the Chittaurgarh line was connected to Jodhpur via Marwar. The 152 kilometre route ascends the plateau in a spectacular climb known as the "ghat section", meeting the Chittaurgarh line at Mavli Junction. Marwar Junction receives a brief mention at the beginning of Kipling's *The Man Who Would Be King* as the place where the narrator first meets Daniel Dravot – the aspiring monarch of the title – as he plans to blackmail a local ruler by impersonating a newspaperman. By the end of the tale, Dravot has met an unsurprisingly sticky fate. When the princely states finally met their own end in 1947, Mewar was one of the first to join the union.

Today only the Mavli-Marwar section and a short run from Mavli to Bari Sadri remain of the metre gauge network, with the Jodhpur-Marwar and Udaipur-Chittaurgahr sections converted to broad gauge. There is no longer a freight service, and two passenger

trains a day make the run from Mavli to Marwar and back again, carrying locals to their villages and pilgrims to the shrine of Srinathji at Nathdwara. The train also passes the shrine of Eklingji, where Bapa Rawal had the kingdom of Mewar bestowed on him. A metre gauge line was built to connect Udaipur to Ahmedabad in Gujarat in the 1960s, and is slated for conversion to broad gauge. It runs through spectacular landscapes for 100 or so kilometres south of Udaipur, up to the town of Dungarpur. This and the Mavli-Marwar section are great favourites with rail enthusiasts, saved so far from conversion by their rugged and beautiful surroundings.

Page 77–8: Padla, 14 August 2006
Above: Udaipur to Zawar, 25 March 2011

Left: Phulad, 15 August 2006

Right: Semi-nomadic Raika tribesman, Marwar, 15 August 2006

Above: Udaipur, 25 March 2011
Right: Kambli Ghat, 14 August 2006

Left: Kankroli to Marwar, 15 August 2006
Right: Kambli Ghat to Goranghat,
14 August 2006

Left & above: Kambli Ghat to Goranghat, 14 August 2006

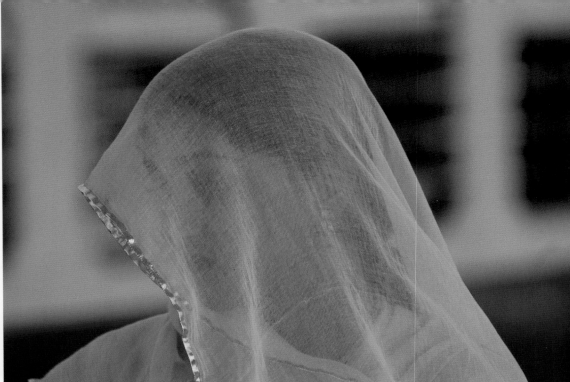

All: Phulad to Marwar, 15 August 2006

THE KANGRA VALLEY RAILWAY

THE KANGRA VALLEY RAILWAY

DELHI

Gauge: Two feet
Length: 164 kilometres
Location: Punjab and Himachal Pradesh
Route: Pathankot to Jogindernagar via Palampur
Elevation: 32–1210metres
Year of completion: 1929

Converted by European settlers into a rich tea-growing district, the Kangra Valley stretches beneath the Dhauladhar foothills of the Western Himalayas. Unlike its neighbouring railway the Kalka-Shimla, however, the Kangra Valley railway's provenance was one of industrial functionality, built to move heavy equipment to the Shanan hydro-power project near Jogindernagar. It was also intended to provide a transport link to the important temples in the area including Jawalamukhi, Brajeshwari, Chamunda Devi and Baijnath, and to towns including Kangra, Dharamshala and Palampur. According to rail historian RR Bhandari the construction was a financial disaster: a proper survey was not undertaken and the budget escalated to Rs 296 lacs from an initial projection of Rs 134 lacs, and it is said that the line has never returned a profit. The upper section, between Baijnath and Jogindernagar, was torn up in 1941–2 and the rails shipped to the Middle East for use in the Second World War. The section was rebuilt after Independence and reopened in 1954. In 1973, 26 kilometres of the track were realigned to allow for the inundation of Pong Reservoir.

 Road and rail run parallel to one another for the first 21 kilometres of the line until the track veers south-east to meet Guler and then begins its steady ascent through the settlements of Jawalamukhi Road, Kangra, Palampur and Ahju, the highest point of the line at 1,210 metres above sea level. It is between Baijnath Paprola and Ahju that the line has its steepest gradient: 1 in 19 for 700 feet at mile 88 with approaches of 1 in 31 and 1 in 25. With only two tunnels – one 250 feet and the other 1,070 feet in length – the snow-capped peaks of the foothills are rarely hidden from the traveller's view as the track hugs the lower contours of this lofty, verdant valley. That the railway is a feat of engineering excellence is no understatement. Whilst tunnels may be few, the line boasts a total of 971 bridges. The construction of the Reond Nullah Bridge evoked rapturous awe in the writers of a 1928 NWR report: "Here took place a titanic struggle between the forces of nature and the ingenuity of science…". This, indeed, might describe the ambitious endeavour of the Kangra Valley railway in all its dogged absoluteness: for slips and landslides and persistent heavy rains have done nothing to curb its determined 85-year-old journey.

Page 90–1: Dhauladhar foothills from Jogindernagar,
16 April 2007

Above: Reond Nullah bridge, 16 April 2007

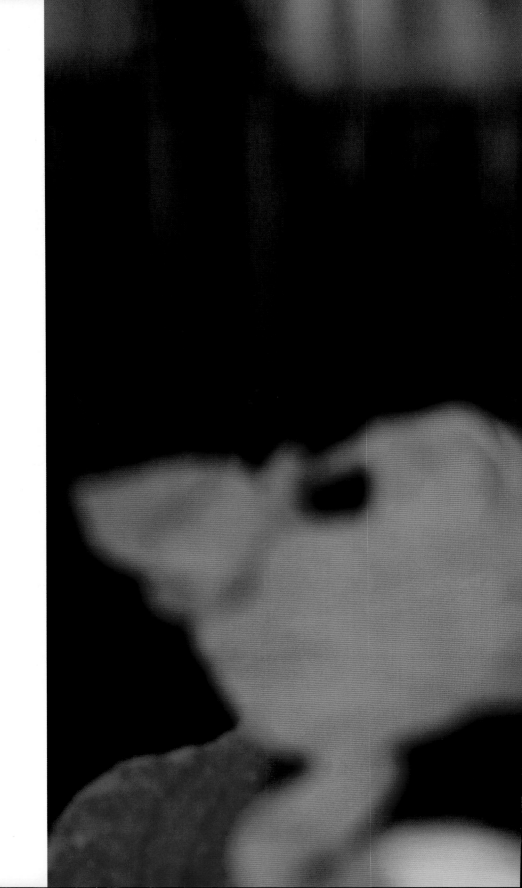

Right: Wedding party at Palampur,
16 April 2007

Above: Kangra, 16 April 2007

Above: Stationmaster's office, Palampur, 16 April 2007

Page 98–9: Reond Nullah bridge, 16 April 2007

Page 99: Ahju, 7 April 2007

Above: Gaddi shepherd cradles lamb at Ahju, 16 April 2007

Right: Haripur Guler, 6 April 2011

Above: Tea-time at Baijnath Paprola, 16 April 2007

Above: Parafin lamps, Baijnath Paprola, 16 April 2007

Page 104: Kangra, 16 April 2007
Page 104–5: Jogindernagar, 16 April 2007
Above & right: Palampur, 16 April 2007

NORTHERN RAILWAY
WELCOME TO CITY OF TEMPLES
BAIJ NATH PAPROLA

RLY EMPLOYEES COMMING FROM ALL OVER INDIA. CAN ENJOY BLESS OF NATURE
AND BLESS OF GOD SHIVA. BY STAYING IN OUR HOLIDAY HOME,
RATES —: FOR CLASS III EMPLOYEES FOR EACH DAY Rs —12/-
   "   FOR RETIRED CLASS III EMPLOYEES FOR EACH DAY Rs -25-
   "   FOR CLASS IV EMPLOYEES FOR EACH DAY Rs - 5 /-
   "   FOR RETIRED CLASS IV EMPLOYEES FOR EACH DAY Rs -12/-

BOOKING AUTHORITY
I.O.W. N.R. PALAMPUR
(H.P)

FOR DETAIL CONSULT WITH STATION MASTER ON DUTY.

(THANKS)

178
ZDM₃

 CHITTARANJAN LOCOMOTIVE WORKS

Left: Kangra, 16 April 2007,
Above: Baijnath Paprola, 16 April 2007
Page 110–1 left & right: Palampur, 16 April 2007

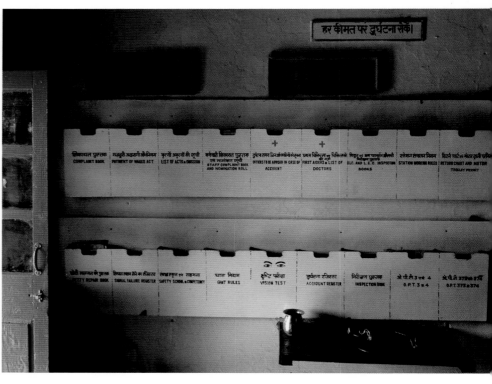

21·38 21·40 बैजनाथपपरोला " " 8PB 21·38 21·40 BAIJNATHPAPROLA "

बिना टिकट यात्रा करना सामाजिक बुराई है।
TICKET LESS TRAVEL IS A SOCIAL EVIL.

वाहर
← OUT

Page 112–3: Bathu Khad bridge, 6 April 2011
Above: Young bucks at Panchrukhi, 16 April 2007

Above: Gaddi women, Palampur, 16 April 2007

" Sadhus swathed in yellow, pink and saffron join at Baijnath Paprola. A sweeper sweeps the carriage floor, already covered in dirt, dust, sweet-wrappers, biscuit packets and discarded newspapers. Extra carriages are added as passengers break out chapatis and sabji from big plastic tiffins. **"**

Above: Level crossing between Jogindernagar and Baijnath Paprola, 16 April 2007

Right: Sadhus, Baijnath Paprola, 16 April 2007

Page 118: Schoolgirls cross the tracks at Kangra, 16 April 2007
Page 119: Samloti, 16 April 2007
Right: New Gaj bridge over the Gaj Khud, 16 April 2007

THE DABHOI RAILWAYS

THE DABHOI RAILWAYS

Gauge: Two feet six inches
Length: 230 kilometres (approx)
Location: Gujarat
Route: Dabhoi-Miyagam, Dabhoi-Chandod
Miyagam-Malsar, Miyagam-Motikoral
Pratapnagar-Jambusar, Kosamba-Umarpada
Year of inauguration: 1862

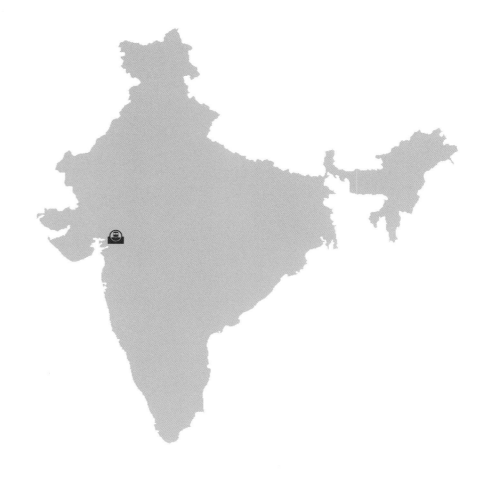

Dabhoi, it is said, was once the busiest narrow gauge junction in the world. A 1500-year-old trading town some 30 kilometres distant from the state of Gujarat's third-largest city of Baroda, it now languishes in dusty obscurity. But it has had its moments of glory. In 1862, when the American Civil War caused a worldwide shortage of cotton, Dabhoi caught a commercial wave when it became the terminus of India's first narrow gauge railway. The 32 kilometre track linked the rich cotton-growing district to the new broad gauge line at Miyagam, giving access to Bombay and the world. It was an experiment, and yet it is evidence that India's narrow gauge railways - so often associated with the British and their hill stations - were actually a local innovation. It reveals also a ruling elite that were progressive: eager to open up a rich hinterland to development, the Gaekwad ('protector of cows', or maharaja) of Baroda decided on rail because the roads became impassable in the rains. Three steam engines were imported but the original line, built with thirteen-pounds-per-yard rails, was not strong enough to support them. So for the first eleven years the trains were drawn by bullocks.

In 1873 it was converted to steam. It was the opinion of the British to utilise 55 pound rails, but the Gaekwad decided that 30 pounds would be sufficient. And so

India's first narrow gauge network was built, not to help colonials escape the heat, but as a hard-headed investment in the future. The Illustrated London News approved. "A native prince has at last constructed a railway at his own cost, and has thus, we may hope, inaugurated the investment of native capital in great public works," its correspondent exulted, even if his impatience was a little uncalled for – the pioneering Ffestiniog narrow gauge railway in Wales only began to use steam in 1863.

Eventually five lines ran from Dabhoi, including a connection to Baroda. Cotton, grain and mogra – jasmine flowers – were the main cargo, but there were other incentives too. An extension was built to Bhadarpur to fetch stone for the Gaekwad's palace, and another to the Narmada River at Chandod, a pilgrimage site. But the railway was just one innovation among many. Sayajirao Gaekwad, who ruled from 1875 to 1939, introduced universal free primary education, founded worthy institutions including a bank and a library, and gave jobs to national leaders including Dadabhai Naoroji and Dr Ambedkar. If Dabhoi today is a backwater, Baroda is one of India's most important centres of finance and industry.

Page 122–3: Signalling the shunting, Chandod, 18 March 2011

Above: Nada to Karjan, 18 March 2011
Right: Kayavardhan to Nada, 19 March 2011

Page 130: Miyagam (top), Choranda Junction (bottom), February 2007
Page 131: Atladra (top), Miyagam (bottom), February 2007
Above: Chandod, 18 March 2011
Right: Masar Road, 20 March 2011

Page 132–3, left & right: Pratapnagar to Jambusar, 21 March 2011
Left: Jal muri, Choranda Junction, 20 March 2011

Left: Stationmaster Satish Kumar, Choranda Junction, 23 March 2011

Above: Choranda Junction, 20 March 2011
Right: Miyagam to Motikoral, 20 March 20111

Above: Miyagam, 20 March 2011

Above: Nada to Karjan, 18 March 2011

THE SHAKUNTALA EXPRESS

THE SHAKUNTALA EXPRESS

Gauge: Two feet six inches
Length: 189 kilometres approx
Location: Maharashtra
Route: Murtijapur-Yavatmal, Murtijapur-Achalpur
Year of completion: 1903

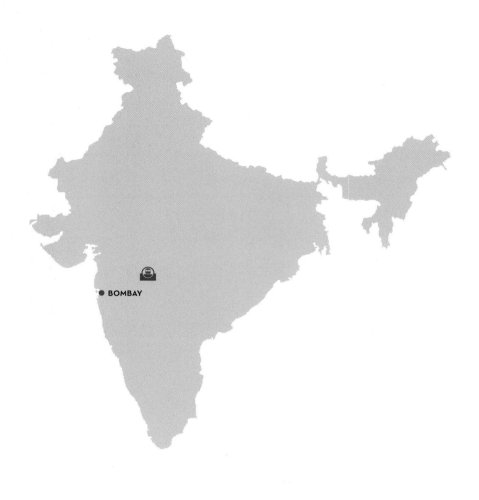

BOMBAY

The Yavatmal to Achalpur railway bisects itself on the line to Bombay at Murtijapur. Elongated coal trains rumble through on the main line at the rate of several an hour, while blue liveried passenger expresses pause fleetingly, jam-packed, on their way to the coast. The track of the Yavatmal and Achalpur service, better known as the Shakuntala Express, lies at the back of the station. The timetable of the Shakuntala Express is about as simple as it gets. Two trains, four carriages each, leave in opposite directions at around seven in the morning. They cheerfully chug their way up to the end of their lines, wait for the engine to be shunted to the other end of the train, and make their way back to Murtijapur.

The name Shakuntala was bestowed on the service years ago by a politician, but the "express" part is a bold flight of fancy. The trains stop at every station, including the many that are abandoned. It takes about four hours to cover the 76 kilometres north to Achalpur, and about six to reach Yavatmal, 113 kilometres to the southeast. In spite of being the only traffic on the line, the trains are often an hour or two late.

The railway was part of a surge of narrow gauge construction which took place around the turn of the twentieth century. Eager to open up further swathes of India to commerce but with limited finances, the central government offered tax concessions to private companies to build railways that would connect to the broad gauge network. The policy resulted in a number of short lines servicing coalfields, sugar mills and plantations, several of which straddled the main line to the east and west of Murtijapur.

The Shakuntala line was built by the Central Provinces Railways Company, floated by Bombay-based conglomerate Killick Nixon & Company, to haul cotton to the broad gauge track. It is widely believed that the line is leased by a British company and operated by the Indian Railways, which returns a fixed percentage of earnings each year. Killick Nixon is largely Indian-owned, but doubts about its ownership echo doubts about its future. With the line in disrepair, locals believe it may close any day.

The track was originally planned to reach the hill station of Chikaldara, another

30 kilometres from Achalpur, but the coming of road traffic scuttled the idea. The guard says that the service is now mostly used by Korku and Gond people, forest dwellers who come from beyond the railhead for seasonal work, harvesting crops of chickpeas, oranges and wheat. The train once hauled teak, but nowadays tribal women gather bundles of firewood which they hook from the windows to sell to slum dwellers in Murtijapur.

Page 142–3: Inspecting the engines, Murtijapur, 3 February 2007

Above: Murtijapur to Vilegaon, 31 January 2007

Above: Motibagh, 3 February 2007
Right: Derelict sidings, Warudkhed, 31 January 2007

Above: Karanja to Karanja Town, 31 January 2007
Right: Ticket sales at Yavatmal, 1 February 2007

Left: Bhadsivni to Vilegaon, 1 February 2007
Right: Vilegaon, 1 February 2007

Left: Murtijapur, 31 January 2007
Above: Karanja Town, 31 January 2007

Left & right: Palash, 3 February 2007

Above: Bullock cart crossing at Motibagh, 3 February 2007
Right: Scooter crossing at Motibagh, 3 February 2007

THE KALKA-SHIMLA RAILWAY

THE KALKA-SHIMLA RAILWAY

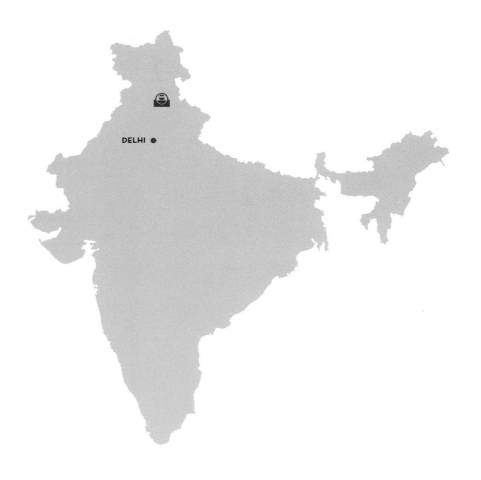

Gauge: Two feet six inches

Length: 96 kilometres approx

Location: Haryana and Himachal Pradesh

Route: Kalka-Shimla

Elevation: 656m-2075m

Year of completion: 1903

Cost: Rs 1.75 crore (17.5 million)

The Kalka-Shimla Railway was built to improve transport to Simla (now Shimla), which had been named the summer capital of British India in 1864. In a gigantic annual operation, the bureaucracy of the Indian government shifted into the hills at the beginning of each hot season, a distance of over 1500 kilometres from Calcutta. The journey was shortened considerably when the capital moved to Delhi in 1911.

The broad gauge link from Ambala to Kalka was built in 1889–91 by the Delhi-Ambala-Kalka Railway Company, and a contract was signed in 1898 for the same company to build a two foot gauge railway from Kalka to Shimla. Construction was already underway when in 1901 it was decided to alter the gauge to two and a half feet on the advice of the military. The line was opened to traffic in 1903.

The railway is notable for its extensive bridging and tunnelling works – when it opened it included more than 100 stone lined tunnels and over 800 bridges. Several of the bridges are multi-arched and built of stone, resembling Roman viaducts, while the longest tunnel, at Barog, is over 1100 metres. The engineer in charge of digging the Barog tunnel is said to have shot himself when the two shafts failed to meet in the middle of the mountain. Because of high capital and maintenance costs and its strategic importance, in 1905 the railway was taken over by the central government. Shimla has remained an important centre since Independence, first as capital of Punjab, then from 1966 as capital of Himachal Pradesh, and the railway has been in constant use. The bureaucracy is as dominant as ever, as seen opposite with the use of a triplicate form, carbon paper and two clerks to issue a 12 rupee ticket.

Trains were originally hauled by converted locomotives from the Darjeeling Himalayan railway, but these were soon replaced with more powerful engines. The Kalka-Shimla Railway has always boasted a variety of rolling stock, catering to all classes of passengers. Today these include railcars – more or less a bus on bogies – deluxe carriages, and a coupe coach with two-person "honeymoon" compartments. The railway remains extremely popular with tourists, not to mention the producers of video abums, and was inscribed in the Mountain Railways of India list of the UNESCO World Heritage register in 2008.

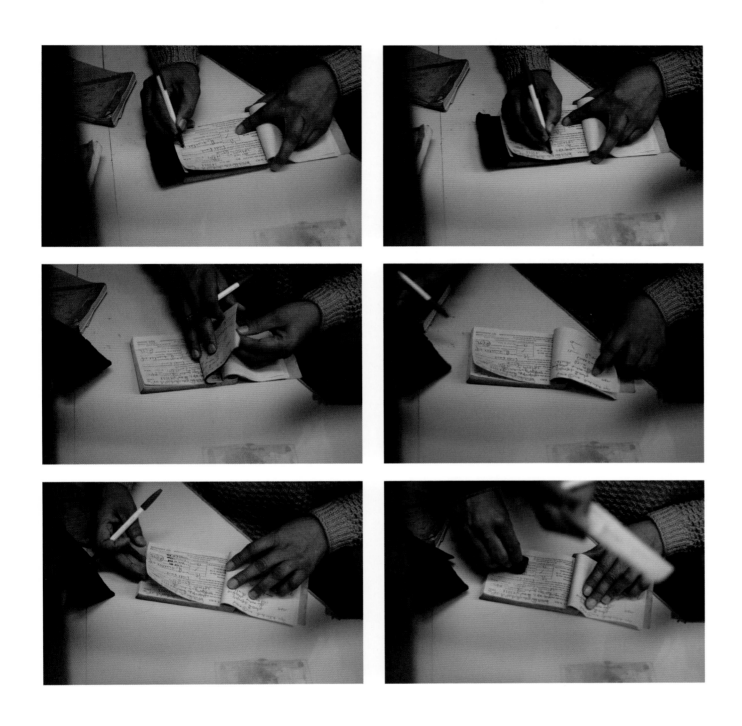

Page 158–9: Samosa waiter at Barog, 8 March 2007
Above: Kalka, 8 March 2007

Above: *Chai stall at Kalka, 8 March 2007*
Right: *Tara Devi to Shoghi, 8 March 2007*

Above: Shimla, 8 March 2007
Right: Mail service at Kalka, 8 March 2007

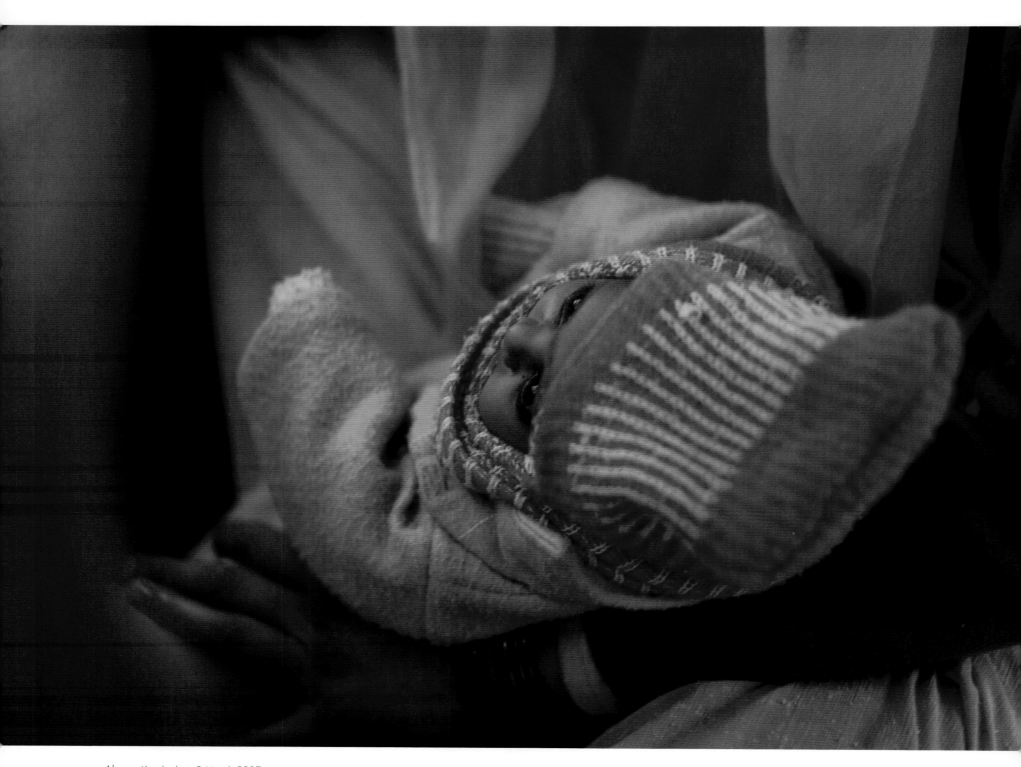

Above: Kandaghat, 8 March 2007
Right: Kalka, 8 March 2007

" Terraced fields appear on the ridges above and I fast begin to feel the mountains. I can smell eucalyptus and see the tracks two points below us twisting around the pink-washed three-storey government residences. The sky bleaches the forest a luminous green. "

Left: Dharampur to Kumarhatti, 8 March 2007.

Above: Tara Devi to Shoghi, 8 March 2007

Page 170–1: Barog tunnel, between Solan and Kumarhatti, 8 March 2007

Left: Barog tunnel, between Solan and Kumarhatti, 8 March 2007

Left, top: Shimla, 8 March 2007
Left, bottom: Kalka, 8 March 2007

Right, top Left: Shimla, 8 March 2007
Right, bottom left: Shimla, 8 March 2007
Right, top right: Kathleeghat, 8 March 2007
Right, top left: Kathleeghat, 8 March 2007

THE MATHERAN
LIGHT RAILWAY

THE MATHERAN LIGHT RAILWAY

Gauge: Two feet
Length: 20 kilometres
Location: Maharashtra
Route: Neral-Matheran
Elevation: 39m-804m
Year of completion: 1907
Cost: Rs 16 lacs (1.6 million)

BOMBAY

The Matheran Light Railway was the idea of Abdul Hussein Adamjee Peerbhoy, the son of Bombay tycoon Sir Adamjee Peerbhoy. It connects the popular hill station at Matheran to the broad gauge line from Bombay to Karjat, built in 1856. Matheran, which means "jungle top", lies on a densely forested plateau at the top of a steep mountain in the Sahyadri range, part of the rugged Western Ghats which cover much of southwestern India. "An insular rock lifted into the firmament" is how a 1910 promotional calendar described the resort, spruiking its curative properties. "It would be difficult to discover on the map of the world a spot so endowed with refreshment and health and peace."

The railway was a driving passion for Abdul Hussein, who personally supervised its construction and lived in Matheran until his death in 1918. The line takes a zig-zag route up the mountainside with a steep gradient and many sharp curves, but no reverses and only one short tunnel. The maximum gradient is one in twenty, restricting speeds to a maximum of 16 kilometres per hour. The final section offers wonderful views of the Sahyadris as the train rounds Mount Barry before diving into the jungle that surrounds the town.

The Matheran railway was entirely funded by the Peerbhoy family, and was privately owned. The consulting engineer on the project was E.R. Calthrop, who had devised a series of acclaimed innovations for the nearby Barsi Light Railway (since converted to broad gauge). According to R.R. Bhandari, workers refused to blast the route for fear of harming the numerous snakes inhabiting the hillside, and the army had to be brought in to complete the work. When it was opened, the railway almost halved the travelling time from Bombay to Matheran. The line was acquired by the Government of India in 1948. Sections of the line were washed away in a deluge in 2005, but it was repaired and operating again in 2007, and is as popular as ever. A handy getaway from teeming Bombay, the resort is famous for its peanut brittle, its car-free streets, and its riding horses with names like "Raja" and "Rolex" stitched to their saddlecloths.

Page 174–5: Fixing the axle bearing in the hot-box, Matheran, 26 March 2011
Above: Western Ghats from Matheran, 26 March 2011

Page 178–9: Neral, 26 March 2011
Above: Aman Lodge, 27 March 2011
Right:: Approaching Water Pipe, 26 March 2011

Page 182–3: Water Pipe, 26 March 2011
(left), Matheran, 27 March 2011 (centre)
Neral, 27 March 2011 (right)

Right: Approach to Matheran, 26 March 2011

Above: Aman Lodge, 27 March 2011
Right: Matheran, 27 March 2011

Above: Water Pipe, 26 March 2011

Right: Peerbhoy memorial at Aman Lodge, 27 March 2011

Above: Neral to Matheran, 26 March 2011
Right: Neral, 27 March 2011

Above: Chai at Matheran, 26 March 2011
Right: Locomotive 550, Neral, 4 April 2007
Page 194–5: One Kiss Tunnel, Neral to Matheran, 26 March 2011

"It is a bone-juddering ride as we steadily ascend and the valley sides drop vertiginously. The engine hisses and burps and growls, and a yellow plate marks each curve. Far below, in a haze, are burnt-off fields. I look down on Neral directly below, a contained package of white and pink boxes, ridges stretching out towards it like cats' paws. We whistle through a black-walled tunnel, raw rock gouged from the mountain, and when we exit I see the snakelike track we have just ascended."

Left: Neral to Jumapatti, 26 March 2011
Right: Neral, 27 March 2011

"The train angles upwards from Neral then does a wriggling traverse of mountains before zig-zagging further. We take a hairpin bend around a sugar-loaf mounded hillock and amble past an image of Ganesh on a giant upright slate. Monkeys — like macaques, but with elongated faces — jump and chase one another as we trundle above the forest, like a canopy of cloud below us."

Left & Right: Matheran, 27 March 2011

THE NILGIRI
MOUNTAIN RAILWAY

THE NILGIRI MOUNTAIN RAILWAY

Gauge: Metre
Length: 46 kilometres
Location: Tamil Nadu
Route: Mettapulayam-Udhagamandalam
(Ooty) via Coonoor
Elevation: 326–2203 metres
Year of completion: 1908

CHENNAI (MADRAS)

The Nilgiri Mountain Railway is the only railway in India to use the Abt rack and pinion system for traction, where a cog wheel below the engine locks onto two offset toothed racks fixed between the tracks. The device assists adhesion and braking on the Kallar-Coonoor section of the line, which is 20 kilometres long with a maximum gradient of one in 12.28.

The idea of constructing a railway from Mettupalayam on the Madras Railway to the tea growing district of the Nilgiris and the hill station of Ooty was mooted as early as 1854. Two proposals to build a line using the Swiss Rigi system were put forward, but both were rejected. In 1885 the Nilgiri Railway Company was formed and made a plan to construct a rack line using the simpler and cheaper Abt system. Construction commenced in 1891, but the company was liquidated before the line could be completed. A new company was formed and the line to the hill station of Coonoor, where the engine sheds are located, was finished in 1899. The section from Coonoor to Ooty was completed in 1908. The line was added to the UNESCO World Heritage list in 2005.

The steam locomotives seen in these pictures are Swiss-built X class engines acquired between the 1920s and the 1950s. That means these engines had been in service for between 50 and 80 years when they were photogaphed. Although this represents a remarkable effort of maintenance, the service was prone to multiple delays as crews struggled to keep the locos working. The problem of replacing these unique machines was addressed in 2011, when four new oil-fired steam locomotives, manufactured in the Southern Railways workshop at Tiruchirapalli, were delivered to Coonoor. The machines are being tried out at the time of writing.

Page 200–1: Watering the engine, Mettupalayam, 26 April 2008
Right: Udhagamandalam (Ooty), 26 April 2008

Left: Cricket at kallar, 26 April 2008
Above: Mettapulayam, 25 April 2008

Left & right: Coonoor, 26 April 2008

Above: Udhagamandalam (Ooty), 26 April 2008
Right: Aruvankadu, 26 April 2008

Above: Locomotive shed at Coonoor, 26 April 2008

Above: Lovedale to Fernhill, 26 April 2008

Left: Tea gardens at Udhagamandalam
(Ooty), 26 April 2008

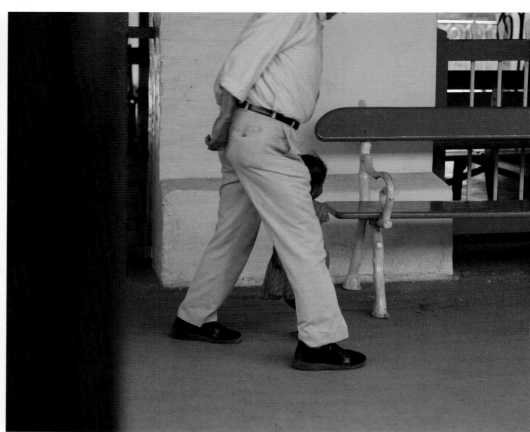

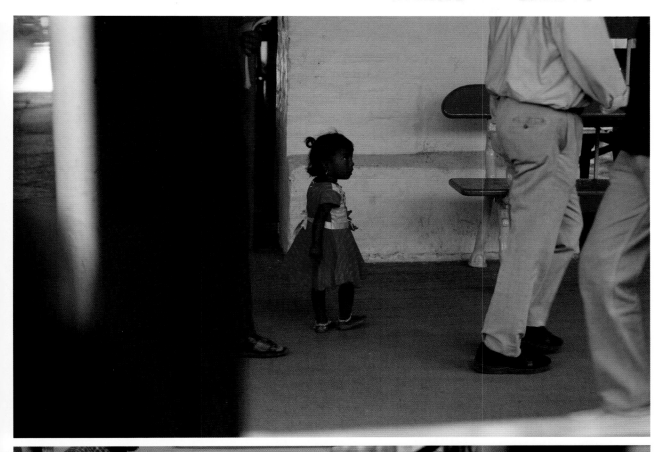

Left: Udhagamandalam (Ooty), 26 April 2008

Left: *Runneymede to Kateri, 26 April 2008*
Above: *Udhagamandalam (Ooty), 26 April 2008*

POSTSCRIPT

The Kangra Valley Railway

The Kangra Valley Railway is the most beautiful railway line in the world. In its six hour ascent, the train grazes fields sunny with mustard flowers or quilted with green wheat. It traces dancing white rivers through boulder strewn gorges, and swings around hillsides fresh with pine and cedar. Mud walled, slate roofed farmhouses flash by, their exteriors washed in ochre or aqua. There are gardens of Darjeeling tea, maroon and gold Tibetan monasteries, and a fort that was prized by the Afghans, Mughals, Sikhs and British. The final, laboured climb tracks the snow-dusted walls of the Himalayas in a glorious slow waltz.

Four important Hindu temples lie sprinkled along the route. About halfway along is a station called Jawalamukhi Marg, the access point for a temple where nine flames issuing from fissures in the rock are believed to originate from the tongue of the goddess Sati. Another version holds that the flames come from the mouth of the local demon Jalandhara, buried under the mountains by the god Shiva. People who've had their prayers answered come here from all over the country to give thanks.

At the station, a cow kneels regally on the platform, a resident herd of goats pesters lunching passengers to share their chapatis, and scruffy sadhus doze in the sun. A friendly Sikh stallholder and his staff of two serve tea and bread pakoras and, when a train is in, work the platform frantically with disposable dishes of boiled chickpeas.

But the stop is 20 kilometres from the temple. Pilgrims cram into waiting jeeps, twelve or more to a vehicle, to travel the rest of the distance to the gold domed shrine, where they will queue for two hours for a brief glimpse of the flame. Locals say that geologists have scoured the hills for years, but have found no sign of natural gas. Further up the line, the train passes the temples of Brijeshwari Devi and Baijnath, and Chamunda, another site associated with Shiva's battle to conquer Jalandhara.

If they've come up from Pathankot, where the line parts from the broad gauge system, the pilgrims have left a grubby town on the plains of Punjab to enter mountains that Hindus regard as the home of the gods, a realm of purity. Almost immediately, they cross a broad river on a narrow bridge, symbolically leaving the sweating plains behind as they enter Himachal Pradesh – the land of snow.

At Haripur Guler, monkeys cruise the platform expecting snacks from pious travellers.

The train trundles past the ruins of Guler Fort, once the capital of a principality which sponsored the important Kangra school of miniature painting, now a mass of overgrown masonry overlooking a jade river. The track passes behind an enormous royal gate which once led to a ferry landing, its sides still decorated with carvings of deities. The land empties to become a lonely expanse of rolling sandstone hills and distant ridges until a silver painted steel bridge crosses the Banganga river. As the girders flash by, travellers get their first view of the Himalayas, a massing presence in the distance, the rocky riverbed pointing the way. This is the Dhauladhar range, a four-thousand-metre-plus wall of grey webbed with white which towers over Kangra. Behind the mountains lie Chamba, Kashmir, Ladakh and, finally, Tibet.

The beauty of the place has an elusive quality, a tension between the warmth of human settlement and powerful forces that would overwhelm it. The lyricism of the farmland is tempered by howling winds and hailstorms from the mountains, and the people are hollow cheeked, leathery. There are no cities here, no big roads, and this small railway seems to fit the scale. It's an epic landscape, a place where nature dwarfs humanity, a place of myth and sainthood. As if to prove the point, the Dalai Lama lives here.

If there's something unworldly about the Kangra Valley Railway, there's also something almost accidental. It was one of the last narrow gauge lines to be built in India, and it probably only came about because of a piece of sloppy accounting. According to rail historian R.R. Bhandari, no detailed engineering survey was done before work began, and construction came to more than double the projected cost – Rs 296 lac (29.6 million) instead of Rs 134 lac (13.4 million). The railway wasn't conceived with passengers in mind – it was built to ship heavy equipment to a hydroelectric project near Jogindernagar, a purpose that lapsed as soon as it was achieved – and the line manages to bypass all the population centres. The stations for Kangra and Palampur are well outside the towns, and the train goes nowhere near Dharamshala. It misses most of Kangra's famous temples by a matter of miles. Ten years after the line was completed in 1929, costs exceeded earnings by a factor of three.

Yet somehow it has survived, withstanding threats of biblical proportions, including flooding and world war. In the early 1970s, the construction of Pong dam and the creation of the massive Maharana Pratap Sagar reservoir inundated part of the line's lower section. Between 1973 and 1976, about 25 kilometres of track was realigned. Travelling the route today when the water is high, the reservoir is a sea of light bordered by velvet fields. When the water is low, the old alignment reveals itself amid the mudflats, along with the ghostly ruin of a temple.

In 1942, the line above Nagrota – about a third of the entire length – was ripped up and shipped to the Middle East for use on military railways. The government relaid the tracks and reopened the section in 1954. Pushing up through the tea gardens of Palampur and finally following a shallow gorge bordered by pine forests up to Jogindernagar, the upper part of the line skirts the base of the Dhauladhar, rolling beneath a sky that is sometimes low and heavy with snow clouds, sometimes icy clear

and immense. Stations are often little more than a shed and a sign with a grassy verge for a platform, and farmhouses huddle, exposed, as if in a Wild West movie.

At Chamunda Marg, a single track halt, a sign says "Alight for Shri Chamunda Temple, Chinmia Ashram, Yol Camp, Dharamsala, Meclotganj". Dharamshala is at least an hour away in a jeep. Chamunda is kilometres away. A small hardship – just enough, perhaps, to remind pilgrims that they are pilgrims.

Jogindernagar, the terminus, is a tiny town straggling along a narrow highway, with a stretch of defunct track leading to the powerhouse. There's something workaday about this railway, something that suggests the virtue of honest labour. Unlike its nearest neighbour, the Kalka-Shimla Railway, the Kangra Valley Railway was built to carry turbines, not shuttle an imperial elite to a summer capital. It lacks the lacy frills and petticoat preciousness of its famous relative, the stone tunnels and viaduct bridges and twee little stations. While the Shimla railway charges into the mountains headlong, the

Kangra railway caresses the contours. Perhaps the intervening years, which brought the Second World War and Gandhi, had taught the empire some humility.

There's only one first class carriage on the Kangra Railway, and you can never be sure which train it's going to be attached to. This is not a train for tourists. Villagers – many of them shepherd farmers of the Gaddi tribe who migrated from Punjab centuries ago – use the railway because they can travel 164 kilometres for 29 rupees, or simply because it happens to pass their village.

The line vaults rivers and streams on bridges made of steel or stone or brick, structures that complement the landscape in an unlikely way. Just past Kangra station, the track leaps a gorge on what a commemorative plaque says is the only steel arch bridge on the Indian railways, a fifty-metre span crossing the sixty-metre deep Reond Khud. Visible only from a few points on the opposite bank, you'd barely know it was there. Village women find it useful as a footbridge.

Kangra station perches on a bluff about five kilometres from Kangra town – home to another famous temple – but lies a little closer to Kangra fort, known for its almost unassailable position atop massive cliffs where a river makes a horseshoe

bend. Considered the key to holding this part of the Himalayas, the fort was taken by Mahmud of Ghazni, one of the earliest Muslim kings to invade India, in the eleventh century, and later by the Mughal emperor Jehangir, then by the Sikh ruler Ranjit Singh, and finally by the British.

But strategically, Kangra is not especially important. It was the kind of place a king would invade to finish off an irritating enemy, or in pursuit of rumoured treasure. It is as much as anything a place of refuge – for the Tibetans now as for the miniature artists who fled here to escape the orthodox tyranny of Aurangzeb in the seventeenth century,

and paint mildly erotic mythical scenes for the raja's court. For most of its thousand year history, the fort lay within the hands of local rulers.

The stronghold is broken now, shattered by an earthquake in 1905, but at night its floodlit walls are still imposing amid the looming hills. Climb it at sunset and you can pick out the train line amid patchwork fields far below, while clouds of green parrots feast on insects and the pink of the dying sun sets the walls of the Dhauladhar ablaze. For a moment you possess what all those long ago invaders fought and died for. Then the caretaker comes to tell you he's closing up, and it has slipped from your grasp.

Page 220: Point levers at Palampur, 16 April 2007
Page 221: Kangra, 16 April 2007
Left: Bathu Khad Bridge, 16 April 2007
Above: Dhauladhar hills from Panchrukhi, 16 April 2007

ABOUT THE AUTHOR

Australian photojournalist and travel writer Angus McDonald was born in Paris in 1962. From his base in Mcleodganj in the Indian Himalayas - home also to His Holiness the Dalai Lama and the Tibetan exile community - his assignments took him across Asia. With his lively style and dry humour combined with a profound respect and compassion for the people, places and rituals he observed, his writing and photography commanded a wide and diverse audience. His photographs and articles have appeared in leading publications worldwide including *The Times, The Guardian, The Daily Telegraph, The Sydney Morning Herald, National Geographic Adventure, Time Asia*, and the *South China Morning Post*. He is the author of *The Five Foot Road: In Search of a Vanished China* (Angus & Robertson) which documented his 1994 journey across China to Burma in the footsteps of Victorian explorer George Ernest Morrison – "Morrison of Peking".

Angus spent three years compiling *India's Disappearing Railways*, travelling to the most far-flung corners of the country; from the Western Ghats of Rajasthan to the Blue Mountains of Tamil Nadu, and from the Himalayas to Assam, this is a tribute to the country he loved and in which he grew up and, as an adult, lived for eight years.

"India's Disappearing Railways celebrates the things that make India great: its tolerance, its diversity, its beauty, its ability to endure. I came to see the survival of these narrow and metre-gauge lines, which one hundred years ago were great feats of engineering, as a symbol of India's ability to improvise and endure, as well as its ability to absorb outside influences and incorporate them into its own being. First, I was drawn to these railways because of the striking beauty of the country; these are some of the most hauntingly beautiful landscapes in the world. Then, as I photographed them, I was struck by the generosity and humour of my fellow passengers. India's disappearing railways are another layer of the country's ancient, rich and diverse culture, representing a slower and more innocent way of life."

Published posthumously and edited by his partner Catherine Anderson – Angus died suddenly whilst travelling in Burma in 2013 – *India's Disappearing Railways* was exhibited at London's Royal Geographical Society in December 2014. All proceeds from his work will go to The Angus McDonald Trust, the charity established in his memory to fund healthcare projects in the remote corners of Asia he documented.

For more information please visit www.angusmcdonaldtrust.org

— *the* —
ANGUS MCDONALD
TRUST
www.angusmcdonaldtrust.org